Constructing Walking Jazz Bass Lines

THE BLUES
IN
12 KEYS
WALKING BASS LINES
FOR
GUITAR

By Steven Mooney

©Waterfall Publishing House 2019

Copyright © WATERFALL PUBLISHING HOUSE LLC 2019

All Rights Reserved
No part of this publication may be produced, stored in a retrieval system or transmitted in any form or means, photocopying, mechanical or electronic without prior written permission of Waterfall Publishing House LLC.

Print Edition 2019.

Print Edition ISBN 978-1-937187-97-2
Ebook Edition ISBN 978-1-937187-96-5

Library of Congress Control Number:

Musical Score : Jazz
Musical Score : Studies & exercises, etudes

Layout and music engraving by Steven Mooney
Cover Design by Steven Mooney

FOREWARD

The Blues in 12 Keys - Walking Bass Lines for Guitar Book I

The Blues in 12 Keys is a complete guide for the guitarist demonstrating the devices used to play walking bass lines and chords in solo or accompaniment settings.
Including
Bebop Blues progression, Minor Blues & Blues with a Bridge, 3 note shell voicings, Chord inversions, Chromatic approach notes, Voice leading, Triads, 7th chords, Harmonic anticipation, Pedal points, Turnarounds, Tri tone substitution.

Part 1. Demonstrates the various techniques used to provide forward motion into bass lines and outlines comping patterns to build a fluid walking bass style for all musical situations.
The exercises build in a stepwise manner and are designed to give the guitarist a solid foundation in the walking bass style incorporating 3 note shell voicings.

Part 2. Expands on the lessons and techniques used in Part 1 providing the guitarist with 60 choruses of examples written out in all 12 keys covering the Jazz & Bebop blues progressions.

Part 3. Blues with a Bridge in 12 keys - Classic blues form of AABA 3 choruses of Blues with a Rhythm Changes bridge. Completely notated with walking bass lines and shell voicings.

Part 4. Minor Blues in 12 keys - includes 24 choruses of notated examples of Minor Blues walking bass lines and shell voicings.

All examples are shown in Guitar Tab and Standard notation.

TABLE OF CONTENTS

PART 1   The Blues in F

The 2 feel walking bass lines - The root & 5th .... p. 8
2 feel walking bass lines - V to I motion .... p. 9
Rhythmic embellishment of the 2 feel .... p. 10
The Jazz Blues progression .... p. 11
The Jazz Blues progression & the application of triads .... p. 12
The 4 feel constructing walking bass lines with triads .... p. 13
Voice leading the Dominant 7th chord .... p. 16
The chromatic approach from below .... p. 18
The chromatic approach from above .... p. 20
Chromaticism and the walk up
and the walk down .... p. 22
Repeated notes and chromaticism .... p. 24
Harmonic Anticipation and playing across the bar .... p. 26
Voice leading & 7th chords .... p. 28
Pedal points .... p. 30
Tri-Tone substitution .... p. 32
The Turnaround .... p. 35
Bebop Major Blues progression .... p. 38

PART 2   The Blues in 12 Keys

Blues in F .... p. 42
Blues in Gb .... p. 44
Blues in G .... p. 47

©Waterfall Publishing House 2019

TABLE OF CONTENTS cont...

Blues in Ab .... p. 49
Blues in A .... p. 52
Blues in Bb .... p. 54
Blues in B .... p. 57
Blues in C .... p. 59
Blues in Db .... p. 62
Blues in D .... p. 64
Blues in Eb .... p. 67
Blues in E .... p. 69

Part 3 Blues with a Bridge in 12 Keys

Blues with a Bridge in Bb .... p. 74
Blues with a Bridge in B .... p. 76
Blues with a Bridge in C .... p. 78
Blues with a Bridge in Db .... p. 80
Blues with a Bridge in D .... p. 82
Blues with a Bridge in Eb .... p. 84
Blues with a Bridge in E .... p. 86
Blues with a Bridge in F .... p. 88
Blues with a Bridge in Gb .... p. 90
Blues with a Bridge in G .... p. 92
Blues with a Bridge in Ab .... p. 94
Blues with a Bridge in A .... p. 96

Part 4 Minor Blues in 12 Keys

Minor Blues in D .... p. 100
Minor Blues in Eb .... p. 101
Minor Blues in E .... p. 102
Minor Blues in F .... p. 103

Minor Blues in F# .... p. 104
Minor Blues in G .... p. 105
Minor Blues in Ab .... p. 106
Minor Blues in A .... p. 107
Minor Blues in Bb .... p. 108
Minor Blues in B .... p. 109
Minor Blues in C .... p. 110
Minor Blues in C# .... p. 111

In Conclusion .... p. 112

To download the playalong backing tracks to this book series or other books by Constructing Walking Jazz Bass Lines
visit
www.constructingwalkingjazzbasslines.com/playalongs-downloads/

Part 1 The Blues in 12 Keys.

2 Feel Walking Bass Lines - The Root and the Fifth

The first example shown below outlines the basic jazz blues progression in the key of F.
The walking bass line technique being shown is the 2 Feel bass line using only the Root and 5th of the chord.
At this stage there is no use of chromaticism or voice leading.
This example is the first in a series of stepwise exercises showing how to construct functional walking bass lines for the guitarist.
This type of accompaniment or comping could be used on the head or first chorus of a solo.

2 Feel Walking Bass Lines - The Root and the Fifth
V to I Motion

The second example shown below builds the forward motion of the bass line by using the device of leading into the chord change by using a V to I motion.

Notice in bar 4 on beat 4 the F natural is the 5th of the Bb 7 chord.

Notice in bar 8 on beat 4 the D natural is the 5th of the Gmin7 chord.

Notice in bar 9 on beat 4 the G natural is the 5th of the C7 chord.

Rhythmic Embellishment of the 2 Feel Walking Bass Lines
The Root and the Fifth

The third example shown below builds the forward motion of the bass line by using the device of rhythmic embellishment.
By placing some of the walking bass line on the upbeat there is now a stronger sense of forward motion or the feeling of the bass line pushing forward.

The actual harmonic function of the bass line is the same as example 2.

The Jazz Blues Progression

In the previous examples the Blues progression being used to construct the walking bass lines has been a simplified jazz blues progression.
In the following examples the chord progression builds to a more common or popular Jazz Blues progression used on gigs.
This progression has a stronger sense of more forward motion due to the device of increasing the harmonic rhythm, eg using 2 chords per measure.

Notice in bar 4 there is now a II V leading to the Bb7 chord

Notice in bar 8 there is now a II V leading to the G min 7 chord

From bar 8 thru 10 the progression is a III VI II V leading to the turnaround in F

The " turnaround " in bars 11 & 12 is now the I VI II V progression leading back to the top in the key of F.

The Jazz Blues Progression and the Application of Triads

In the previous examples the walking bass lines have been constructed using only the root and the fifth.
The next step in the construction of walking bass lines is to incorporate the triad.
The triad consists of the root, 3rd & 5th degrees of the scale or 1, 3, 5 of the chord and provides strong forward motion by outlining the chord and the chord progression.

The following example shows how to construct the diatonic triads off of the F Major scale. Triads are constructed in 3rds and are built from all degrees of the scale as shown in the example below.

F Major Scale

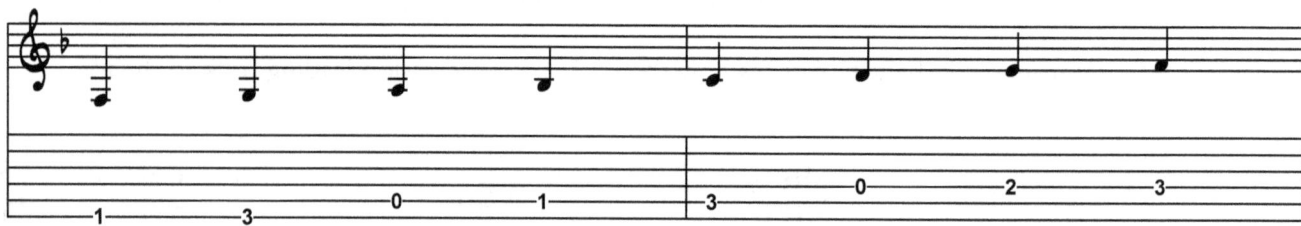

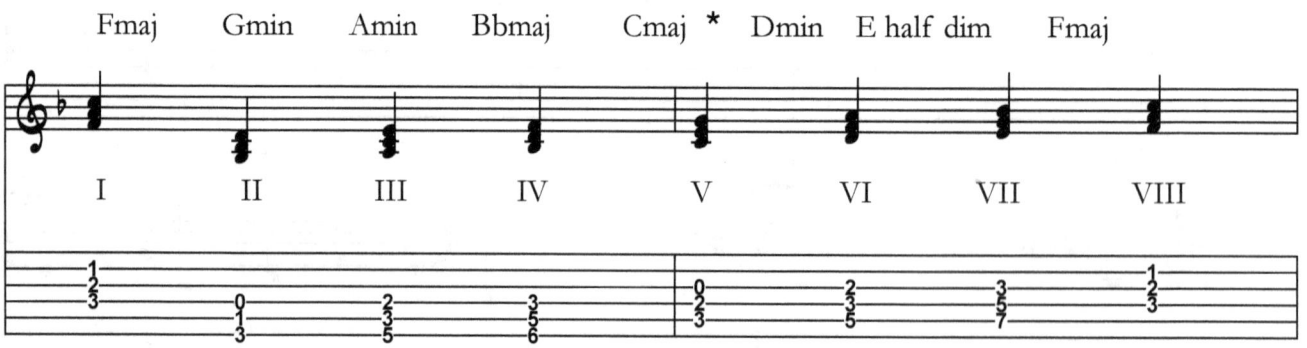

*Notice that the V chord triad is Major, it becomes Dominant when the b7th is added.
The triad notation eg the first F maj triad, has been used in this format to accomodate those using tablature.
The example of building the triads has been offered in the key of F to show how the III VI II V eg (Amin7 D7 / Gmin7 C7) terminology relates to the previous example of the Jazz Blues progression.
The more experienced guitarist or the reader with a knowledge of harmony and theory will be aware that the triads built from the F Dom 7 scale would be different from the example shown above. This is due to the fact that the F 7 chord is derived from the Bb Major scale.
For the purpose of this chapter the example of the Major scale was shown to outline the function of the I chord in relation to the II V and the III VI II V chord.
When playing the Jazz Blues progression shown in these chapters the F 7 chord is functioning as the I chord.

The Jazz Blues Progression
The " 4 Feel " Constructing Walking Bass Lines with Triads

The following examples outline the use of the triad eg. chord tones 1, 3 & 5 when constructing walking bass lines over the Jazz Blues progression.
Notice that there is still no use of chromatic approach notes.
The walking bass line is now using the classic 4 feel or 4 quarter notes per bar. The line and overall sound of the accompaniment really starts to " swing " and we are still only using 3 notes of the triad.

As you start to develop an ear for how you want your lines to sound the possibilities become vast.

The next example continues with a variation of the walking bass line whislt still using only the triad to construct the walking bass line.
Notice that we are now comping on the " and " or up beat of beats 1 and 3.

As with all areas of practice, start slowly to grasp the material striving for even tone and time feel, making sure that each note gets its full rhythmic value.
When the material gets more comfortable, only then increase the tempo.

Trying to progress to quickly without grasping the fundamentals will be time consuming in the long run.

Voice Leading the Dominant 7th Chord

In the following example we are continuing our use of triads to construct the walking bass lines over the Jazz Blues progression.

Notice on the 4th and 6th bar we are introducing the dominant 7th chord.

A voice leading technique will be applied to the bass line on the Dominant 7th chord in the 4th and 6th measures moving the b7th of the Dom 7th chord to a chord tone of the next chord.

Ex 1. bar 4 & 5 Eb the b7th of F7 moves down a half step to D the 3rd of Bb7

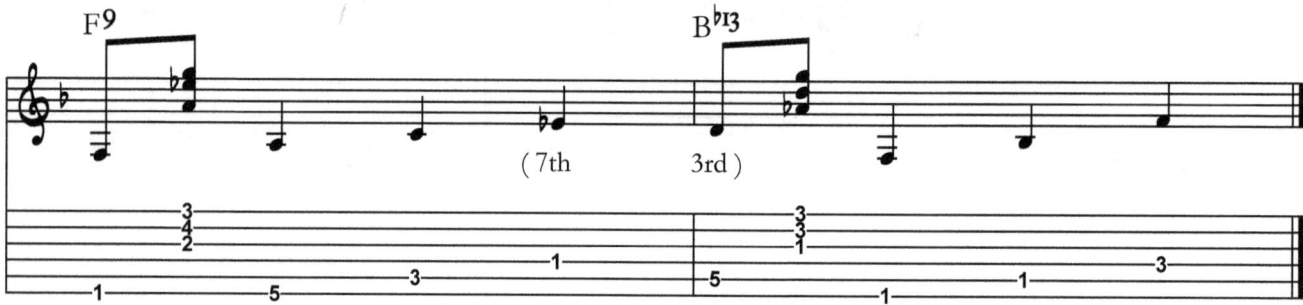

Ex 2. bar 4 & 5 Eb the b7th of F7 moves up a whole step to F the 5th of Bb7

Ex 3. bar 6 & 7 Ab the b7th of Bb7 moves up a half step to A the 3rd of F7

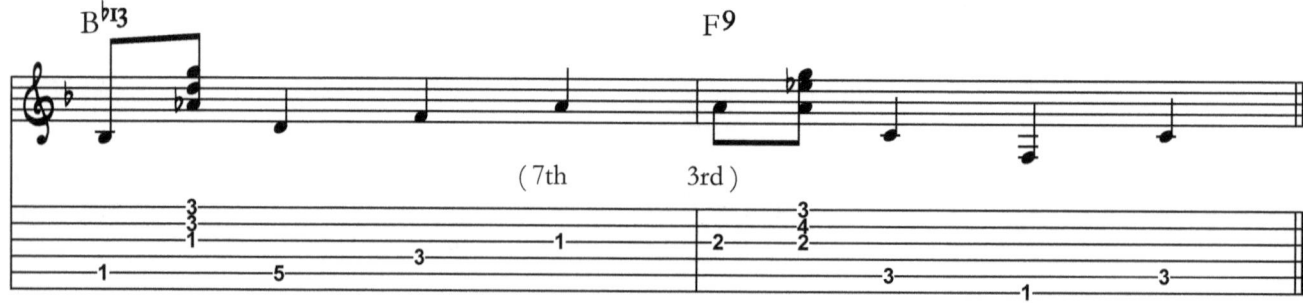

Blues in F Applying the Voice Leading Technique

The Chromatic Approach from Below

In the following example we use the device known as the chromatic approach note.
This example outlines the chromatic approach note a half step below the chord tone. In the following examples we will be using non chord tones.
Chord tones also work well as chromatic approach notes, however for this example we will use chromatic notes not used in the regular chord or scale eg. non diatonic.
This is a very effective technique used to give the line contour and a distinctive sound.
The application of the chromatic approach note and other devices is what gives a particular player " their own sound, " this is what all good musicians are striving for.

Ex 1 Bar 1 & 2 Shows the chromatic approach note C# a half step below D the third of Bb7

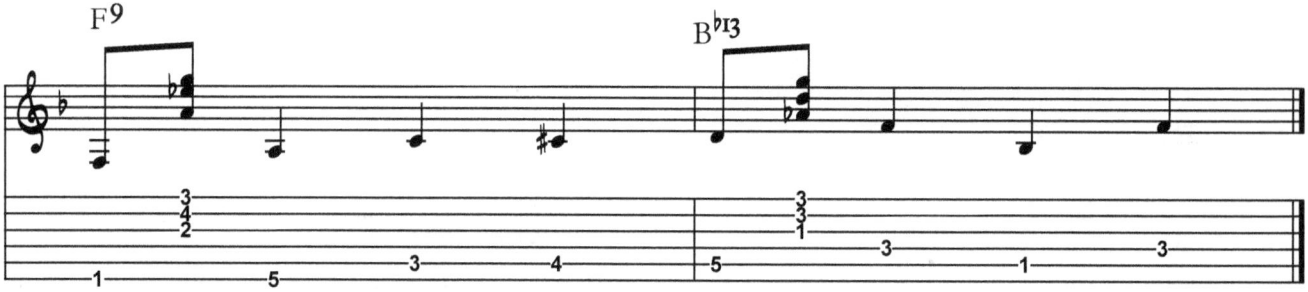

Ex 2 Bar 9 & 10 Shows the chromatic approach note B a half step below C the root of C7

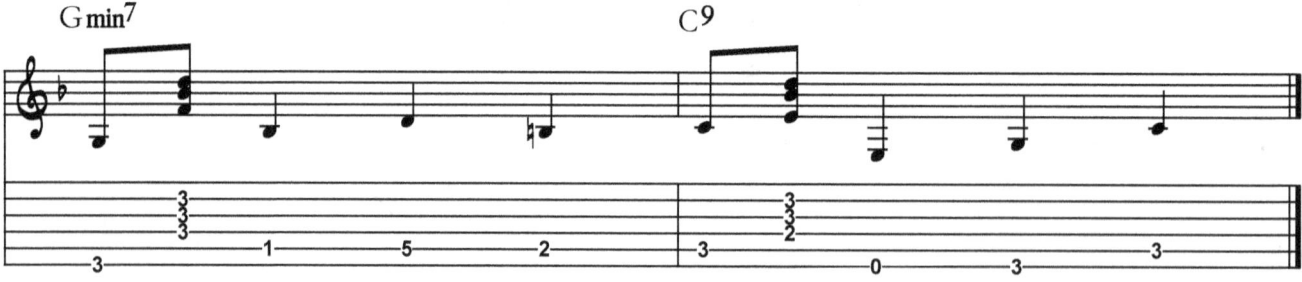

Ex 3 Bar 10 & 11 Shows the chromatic approach note G# a half step below A the third of F7

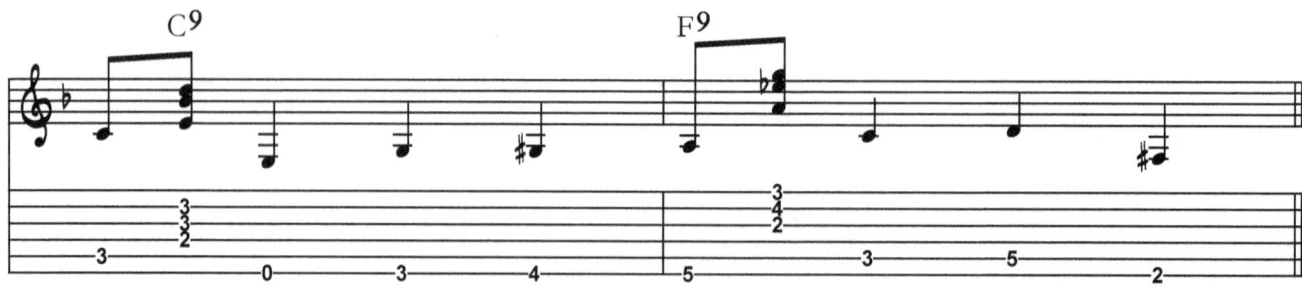

The Blues in F Applying the Chromatic Approach from Below

The Chromatic Approach from Above

In the following example we use the device known as the chromatic approach note.
This example outlines the chromatic approach note a half step below the chord tone. In the following examples we will be using non chord tones. Chord tones also work well as chromatic approach notes, however for this example we will use chromatic notes not used in the regular chord or scale eg. non diatonic.
This is a very effective technique used to give the line contour and a distinctive sound.

Ex 1 Bar 1 & 2 Shows the B a half step above the Bb the root of Bb7

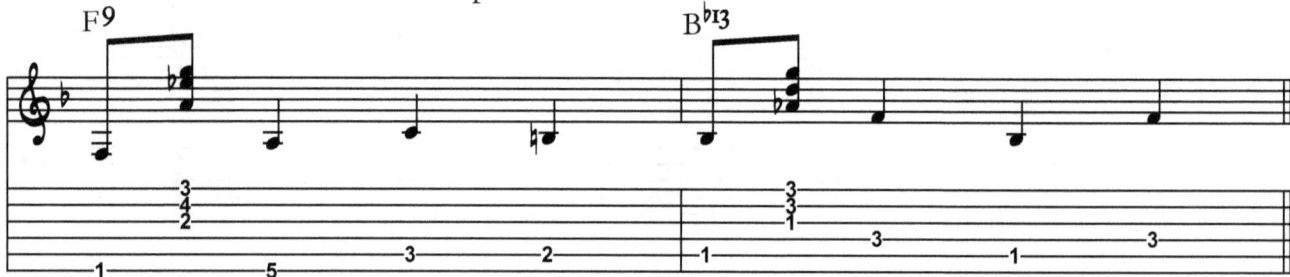

Ex 2 Bar 9 & 10 Shows the chromatic approach Db a half step above C the root of C7

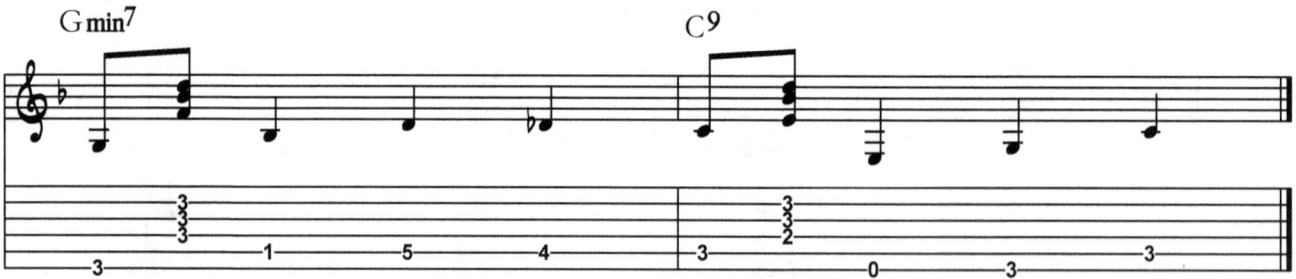

Ex 3 Bar 10 & 11 Shows the chromatic approach note F# a half step above F the root of F7

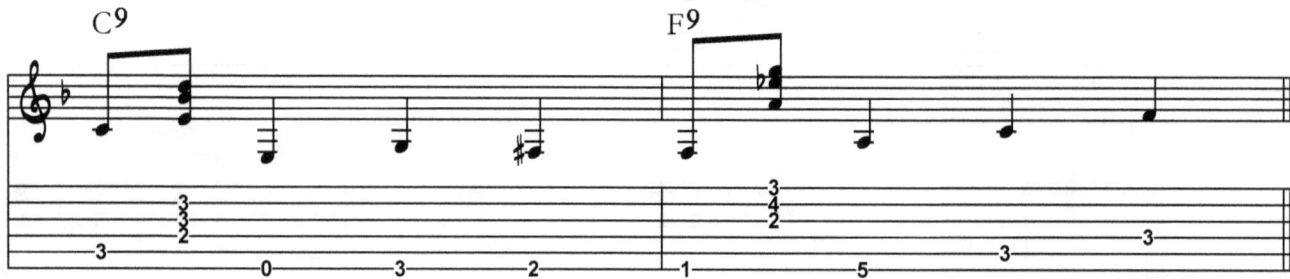

The Blues in F Applying the The Chromatic Approach from Above

Chromaticism ..... The Walk Up & Walk Down

In the following example we continue our approach to chromaticism with two commonly used devices in Jazz walking bass lines.
The Walk Up connects to the next chord change by walking up with two chromatic approach notes.
The Walk down connects to the next chord change with two chromatic approach notes walking down.
This is very strong bass line motion and gives a definite sense of where the line is going.

Ex 1 Bar 2 & 3 Shows the Walk Up, the F 7 is approached by two chromatic approach notes from below the F the root of F 7.

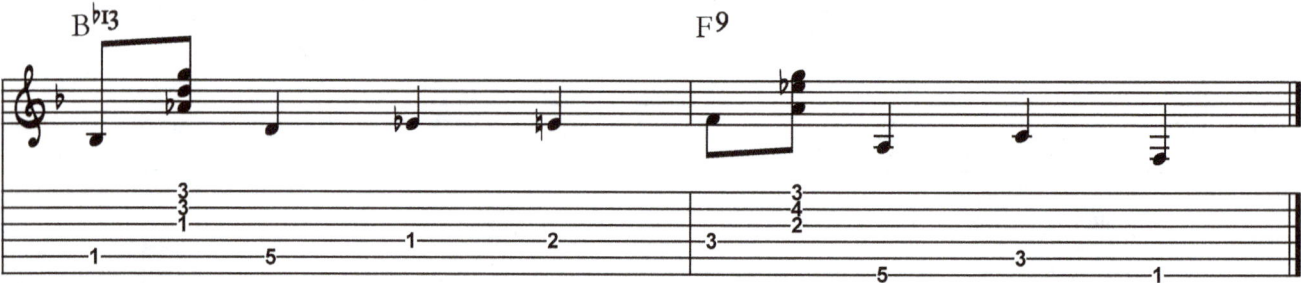

Ex 2 Bar 7 & 8 Here we have the Walk Down, the Amin7 is approached by two chromatic approach notes from above the A the root of A 7.

©Waterfall Publishing House 2019

Blues in F Applying the Walk Up & Walk Down

©Waterfall Publishing House 2019

Repeated Notes & Chromaticism

In the following example we combine our look at chromaticism with the device of repeated notes.

Repeated notes are very effective when the harmonic rhythm increases, eg. two chords per bar. Repeated notes were used extensively in the bebop era as the chord structures developed into two or four chords per bar.

The repeated note gives a strong sense of the harmony being outlined and gives a strong sense of forward motion.

Notice in bar 4 that the progression is now Cmin7 F7, a II V leading to the Bb7 chord, this adds to the harmonic rhythm and is a very common chord substitution used in the Jazz Blues progression.

The Blues in F Applying Repeated Notes & Chromaticism

Notice in Bar 11 that the repeated note is not always the root note of the chord, in this example the 5th is played on beat 1 of the chord eg. an A is played on beat 1 of the D7 chord on beat 3 of bar 11.

Using these devices keeps the bass line interesting by creating a sense of tension and release.

Harmonic Anticipation & Playing Across the Bar

In the following example we look at the technique known as playing across the bar or playing ahead of the changes. The harmony is played for example a beat or half beat early and tied across the bar line. This is another device which gives the bass line a strong sense of forward motion.

When incorporating this technique into bass lines the most important factor to be considered is supporting the melody or soloist and providing a strong foundation.

Ex.1 Here we have bar 3 & 4 of the F Blues progression F7 - Cmin7 F7.
In this example we get to the Cmin7 chord 1/2 beat early.
The bass line anticipates the Cmin7 chord on beat 4 " and " .

Ex.2 Here we have bar 4 & 5 from the F Blues progression.
This time we play the F on beat 4 a common chord tone to F7 and Bb7 . The Bb7 chord is played on the 4 "and " and it is tied over the bar.
In this example we get to the Bb chord half a beat early.

The Blues in F Applying Harmonic Anticipation & Playing Across the Bar

Voice Leading & 7th Chords

In the following example we incorporate 7th chords into our Blues bass line and a technique known as voice leading.

Voice leading is a very effective technique used by all harmonic instruments. Voice leading is a method where a chord tone resolves stepwise to another chord tone of the next chord change. This provides very strong lines and can help to connect the bass line to the chord voicings. Soloists often use this method when constructing guide tone lines.

Ex.1 Shows the progression Cmin7 F7.
Notice that the Bb the b7th of Cmin7 resolves down a half step to the A the 3rd of F7

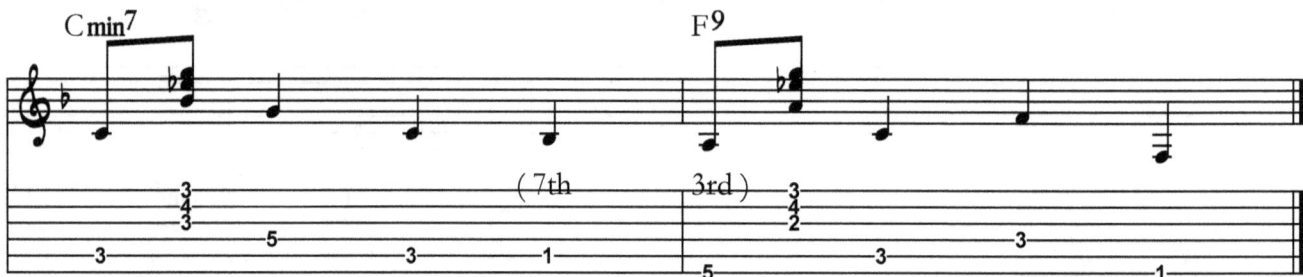

Ex.2 Shows the progression Amin7 D7.
Notice that the G the b7th of Amin7 resolves down a half step to the F# the 3rd of D7

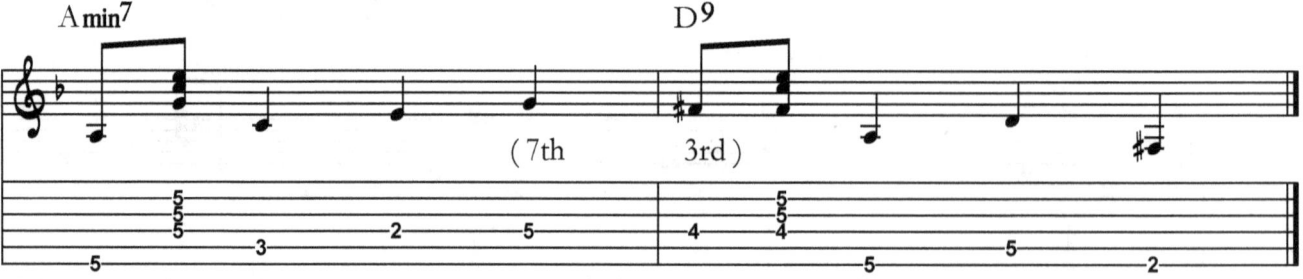

Ex.3 Shows the progression Gmin7 C7.
Notice that the F the b7th of Gmin7 resolves down a half step to the E the 3rd of C7

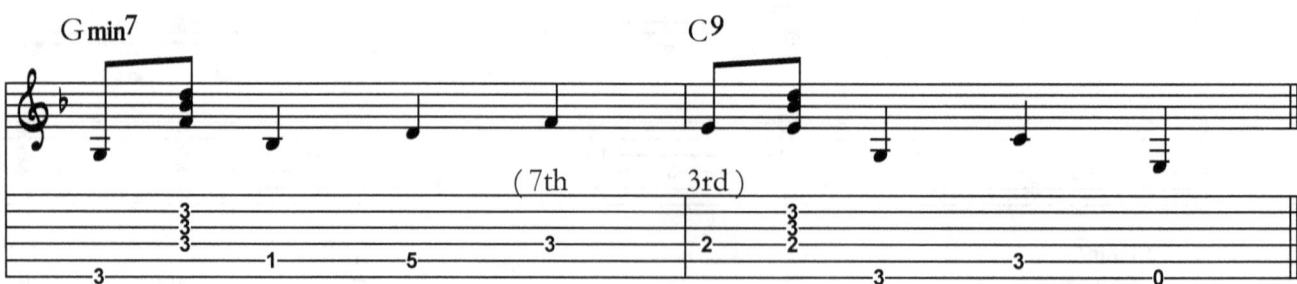

The Blues in F Applying Voice Leading & 7th Chords

©Waterfall Publishing House 2019

Pedal Points

In the following example we look at the technique known as the pedal point.
There are various types of pedal points, the repeated note for an extended number of beats or measures and the rhythmic pedal point.
The pedal point is a device often used to start a tune eg. you might here a horn player say play a pedal on the V chord. A common pedal played in jazz is a pedal on 2 & 4, although there are many types.
Another use of the pedal point is to create tension or a feeling of suspension as one bass note is played throughout a progression of chords, then when the pedal tone is released and the bass goes into walking the changes the tension is released and the music propels forward. This gives the listener the sense that the band is really cookin'.

The Blues in F Applying Pedal Points

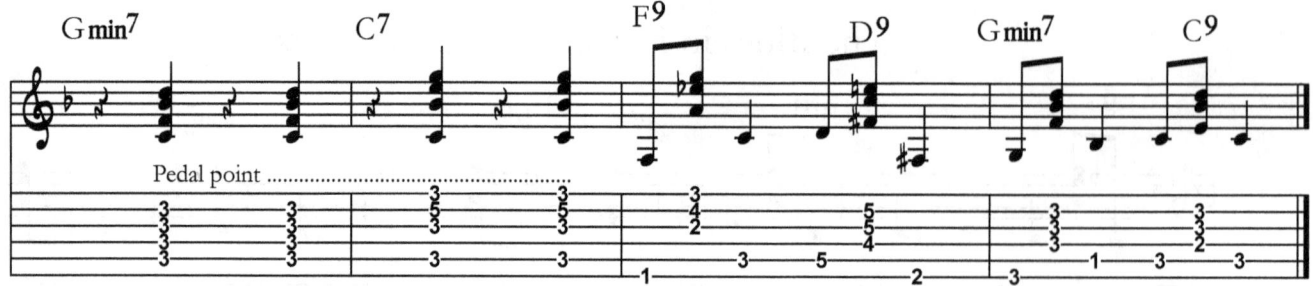

Notice that in the last chorus of the blues there were no chords played over the pedal point in the first 3 measures, this gives a sense of space and variety to the music.
This works because the tonality of the piece had already been established by the previous 2 choruses , this concept wouldnt work so well on the first chorus of a tune unless the music had been previously rehearsed and the soloist was aware of the arrangement.

Tri Tone Substitution

In the following example we look at a harmonic technique known as tri tone substitution. This is another technique used extensively in the bebop era, as well as many others. The tri tone substitute is used to make different chord tensions against the melody or solo and can make the melody sound more interesting or different. This is down to personal taste. The other use of tri tone substitution is to create chromatic bass movement, creating very strong forward motion.
The term tri tone comes from being three tones or whole steps away from the root note.

In the following example we have the progression Gmin7 C7 F7.
A dominant 7th chord can be voiced by playing only the two notes of the tritone interval. In this example the C7 can be voiced as E and Bb.
Using the major 3rd and the b7th.
The sound is immediately identifiable as the dominant 7th sound because of the interval of a tritone.
If we look at the example below and play the common tones from both chords, the E and the Bb we have essentially the same sound using different chords. Eg. C7 & tritone sub Gb7.

©Waterfall Publishing House 2019

In this example we have the tritone substitute of C7 = Gb7. If we count 3 whole steps from the root of C7 eg C - D, D-E, E- F# (Gb) we arrive at Gb our tri tone substitute. Notice that for the Gb7 chord the correct spelling of the b7th should be Fb however E natural is a little easier to read for the beginning to intermediate musician.

The following example shows the common tones from the C7 chord and the Gb7 chord. Eg. the tritone interval.

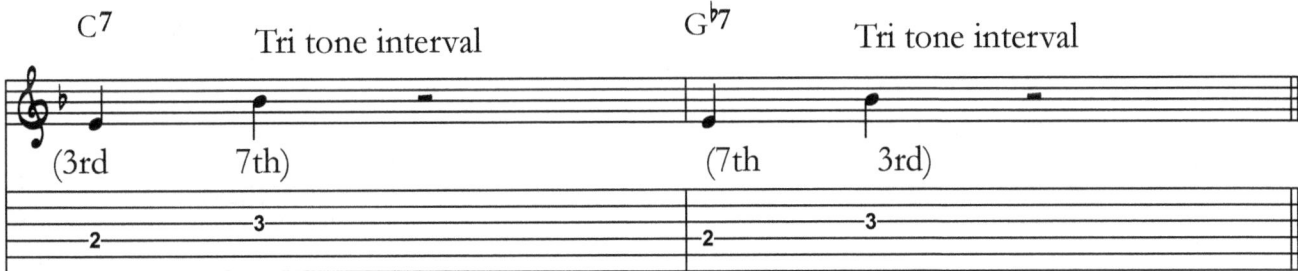

In the following example we look at the II V I progression, in this case Gmin7 C7 F7. Using the tritone substitute the progression now becomes Gmin7 Gb7 F7.
Giving the progression descending chromatic root movement.

In the following example we add the relative II min7 to the tritone substitute eg. Dbmin7 Gb7.

©Waterfall Publishing House 2019

In the following example we condense the progression, giving it greater harmonic rhythm eg. more chords per bar, by keeping the original II V Gmin7 C7 followed by the tritone sub II V Dbmin7 Gb7.

The Blues in F Applying Tri Tone Substitution

The Turnaround

In the following examples we look at the " turnaround ". The turnaround refers to the last 2 bars of the chord progression which leads us back to the top of the form. Quite often you might here someone on the bandstand say, " turn it around " this means start the next tune on the turnaround. Like the pedal point intro, the turnaround intro is very common and can be extended indefinately until the melody comes in.

The most common turnaround is the I VI II V progression, here it is in relation to the Blues in F. In the Blues the I chord is often Dominant as in this example.

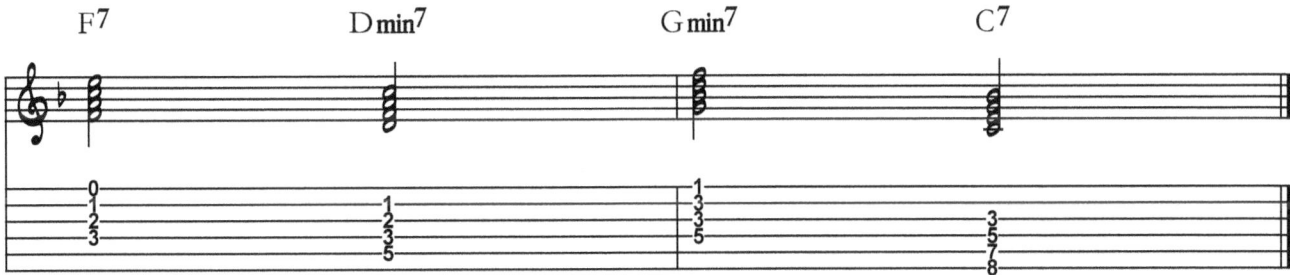

©Waterfall Publishing House 2019

In the following example we substitute the I chord for the III chord, now we have the progression as follows.
Notice in this example the VI chord is a dominant 7 chord. This is because it is functioning as a Secondary Dominant chord eg. V of I eg D7 - Gmin7.

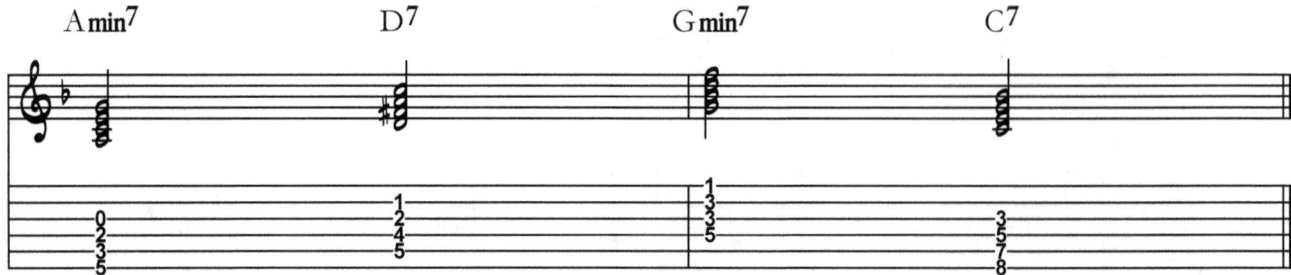

In the following example we apply the tritone substitutes to our turnaround, the progression is as follows.
By applying the tritone subsitutes we have descending chromatic root movement.

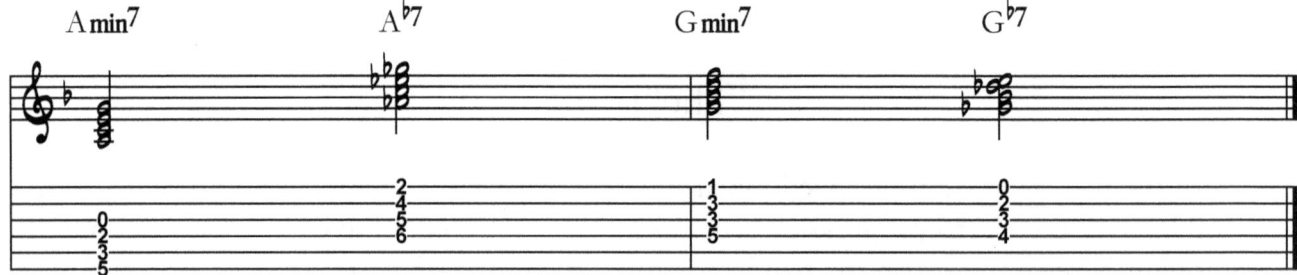

Another common variation on the previous III VI II V example is to make all the chords dominant. This applies the Secondary Dominant principle again.
It gives us what is called a V of V progression . This is the progression used as the bridge in Rhythm Changes.
In the Blues in F our III VI II V turnaround will now be.

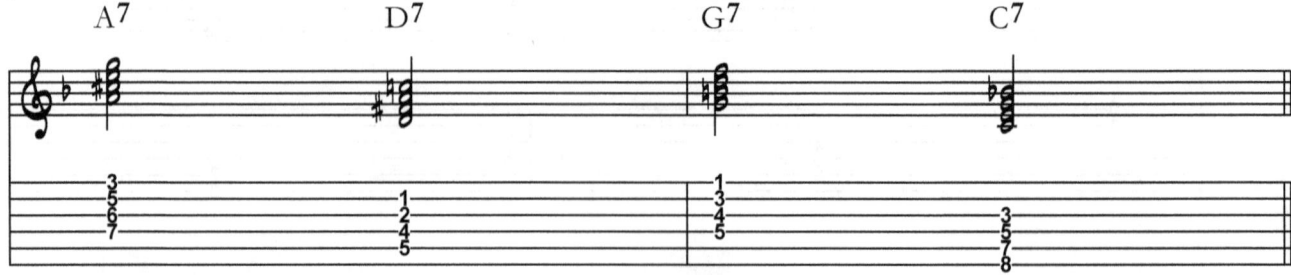

By applying the tritone substitutions to the above progression we arrive at the following turnaround. This is a very common turnaround.

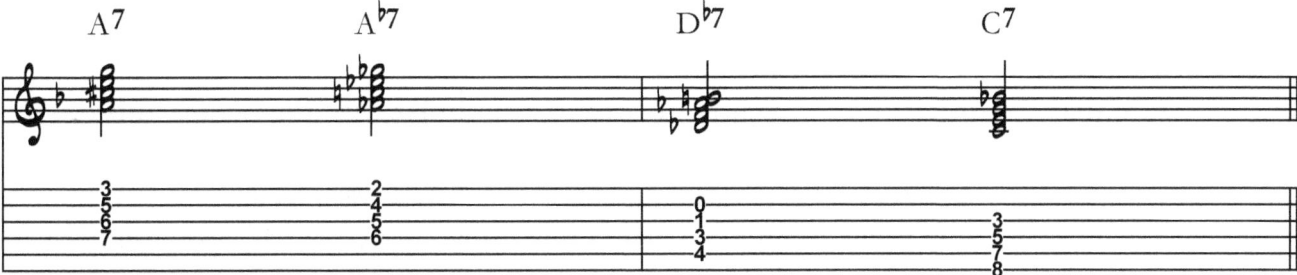

In the following examples we apply the relative IImin7 to the turnaround progression. As you can see the possibilities are vast.

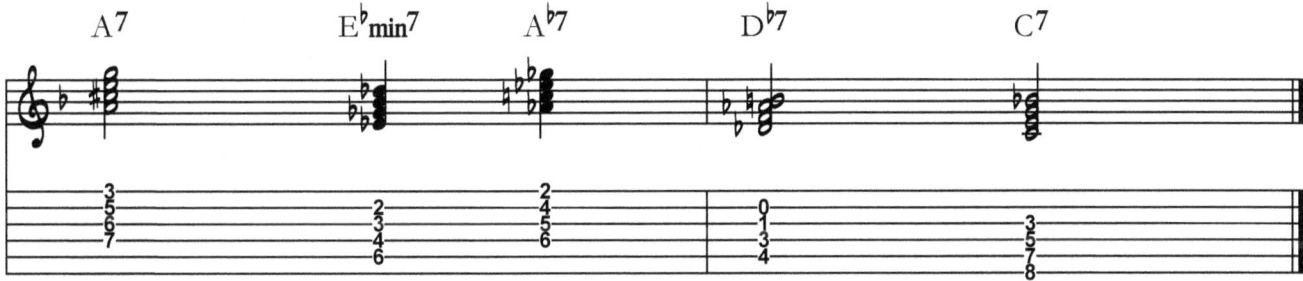

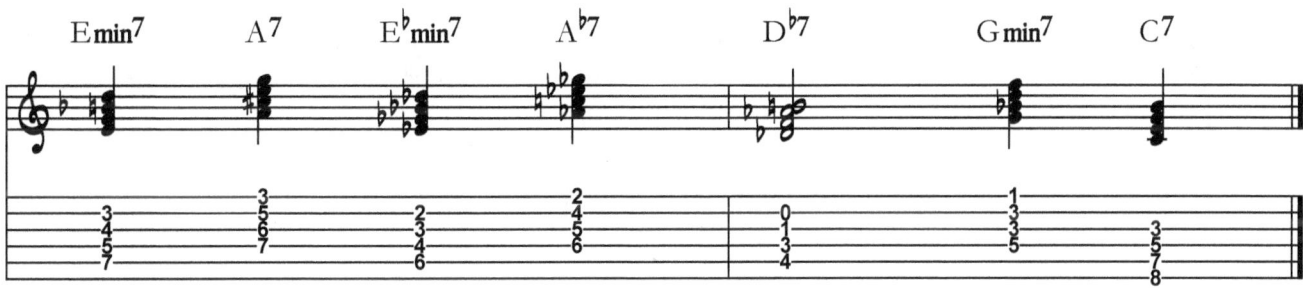

As you can see with the use of the various substitutes there is a lot of variation under your fingers at all times.
Practice the turnarounds in all keys.
As mentioned already you can use the turnaround variations for the intro to tunes as well as applying them to the tags or endings of tunes.

Bebop Major Blues Chord Progression

The next example of the Jazz blues progression is the Bebop Blues or the progression often refered to as " Bird " blues.

Notice that the first chord is a major 7 chord, also popular with the bebop musicians is the 6 chord eg F6.

The tune can be analysed several ways, one of the simplest ways to describe the tune is that it descends from the Imaj7 chord to the IV Dom7 via a series of II V progressions moving stepwise down the scale. eg. F E D C which takes us to the IV chord.

From there the progression uses chromatic II V movement to arrive at the II min7 chord Gmin7.

The rest of the progession is standard Jazz Blues changes.

©Waterfall Publishing House 2019

Part 2   THE BLUES IN 12 KEYS

To summarize the material so far, we have looked at the various devices used to construct walking bass lines in the jazz idiom. Together with the comping options outlined the guitarist now has an understanding of how to combine these two aspects together to make the jazz guitarist sound like two musicians.

The next part of the book deals with the blues in 12 keys and will show examlpes of the Jazz Blues and Bebop blues progression in all 12 keys.

This chapter can be used to help build a bass line vocabulary and will stretch and inspire the guitarist to take their playing to the next level. Moving away from the standard format of having the bass line only on the bottom two strings we will also incorporate the D string into the walking bass line. This will be used as an effect and to make longer bass lines more accesible.

The examples will also in points be " arranged " to have the standard comping and bass line played together for a chorus followed by a chorus of just bass lines without chord accompaniment, followed by a chorus of the standard comping and bass line.
This concept could be used on a gig with a horn or two guitars etc where the comping instrument drops out leaving only the solo voice and bass, only returning to comping to take the head out.

These concepts are put forward so the guitarist has a full range of devices to draw from, freedom comes from being able to make choices.

Blues in F

Blues in Gb

Blues in G

Blues in Ab

Blues in A

Blues in Bb

Blues in B

Blues in C

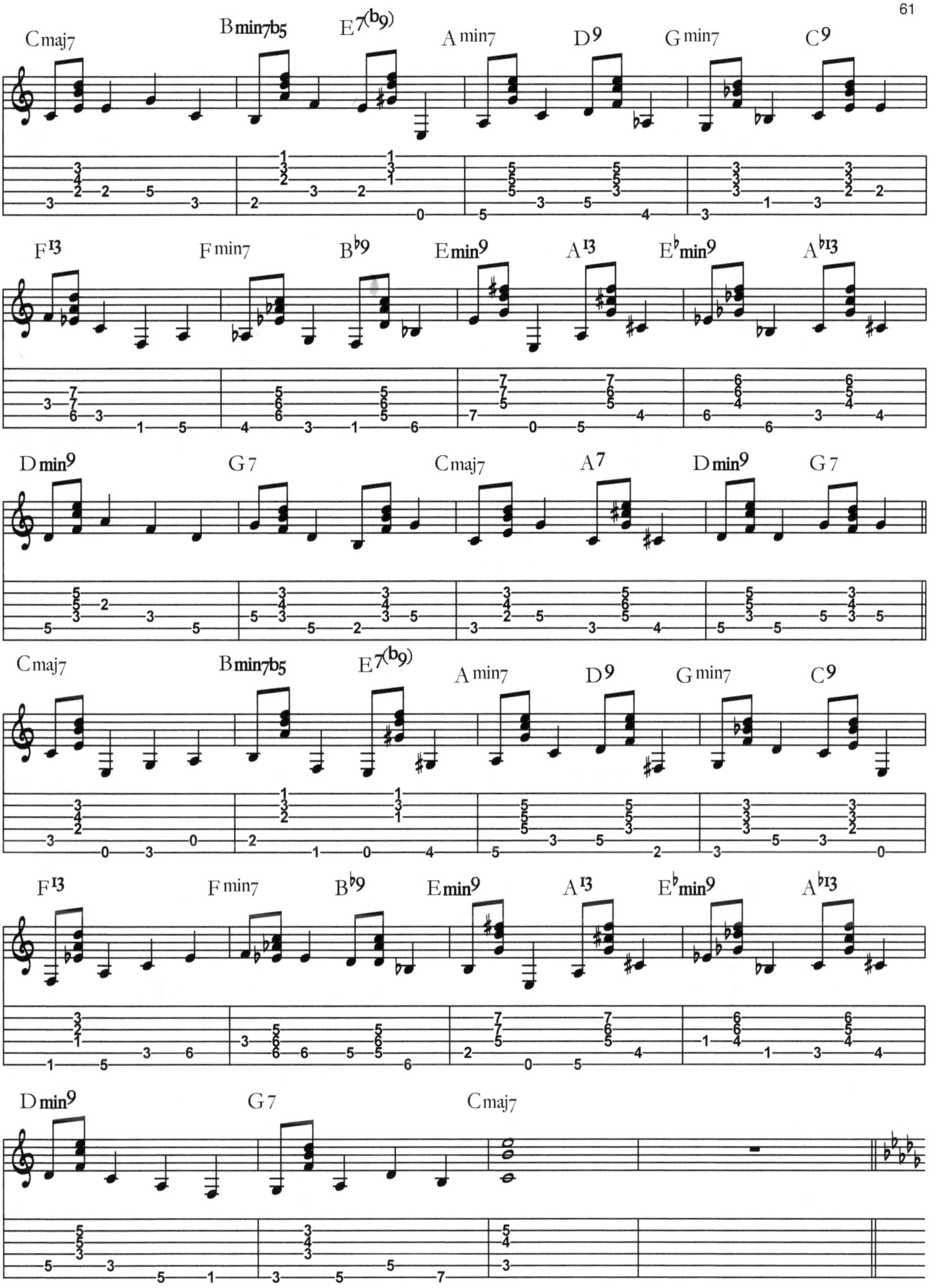
Cmaj7
Bmin7b5
E7(b9)
Amin7
D9
Gmin7
C9
F13
Fmin7
B♭9
Emin9
A13
E♭min9
A♭13
Dmin9
G7
Cmaj7
A7
Dmin9
G7
Cmaj7
Bmin7b5
E7(b9)
Amin7
D9
Gmin7
C9
F13
Fmin7
B♭9
Emin9
A13
E♭min9
A♭13
Dmin9
G7
Cmaj7

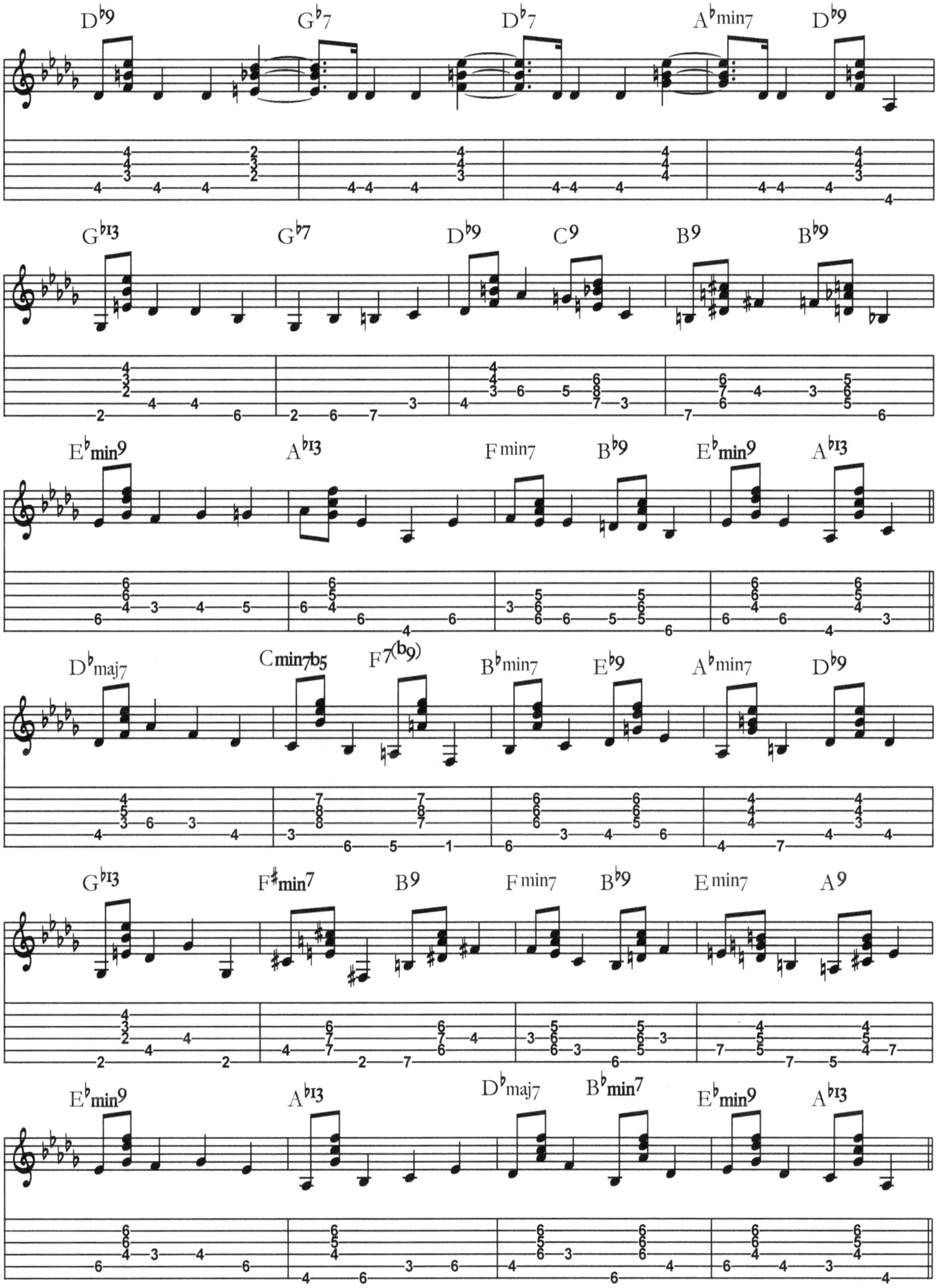
D♭9 G♭7 D♭7 A♭min7 D♭9
G♭13 G♭7 D♭9 C9 B9 B♭9
E♭min9 A♭13 F min7 B♭9 E♭min9 A♭13
D♭maj7 Cmin7b5 F7(b9) B♭min7 E♭9 A♭min7 D♭9
G♭13 F♯min7 B9 F min7 B♭9 E min7 A9
E♭min9 A♭13 D♭maj7 B♭min7 E♭min9 A♭13

Blues in D

Blues in E

©Waterfall Publishing House 2019

Part 3   Blues with a Bridge

The Blues with a bridge is another popular blues progression played by jazz musicians. The form is AABA 12, 12, 8, 12. Quite often the bridge used is a Rhtyhm Changes bridge, although there are many alternatives.

For more information on Rhythm Changes see Book II in this series Rhythm Changes in 12 keys. The form is analyzed in depth with examples of many of the most often used chord substitutions.

Notice the difference in the turnaround between the first and second A sections. This is due to the second A resolving before continuing to the B section. The last A is the same as the first A.

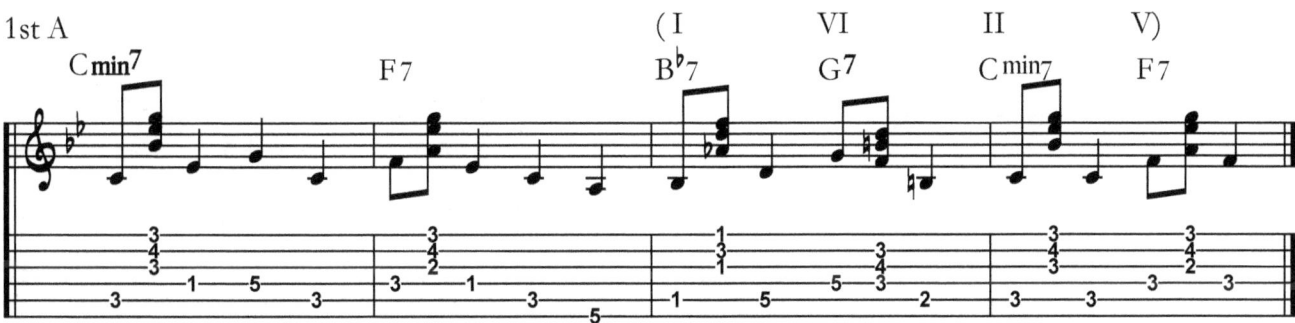

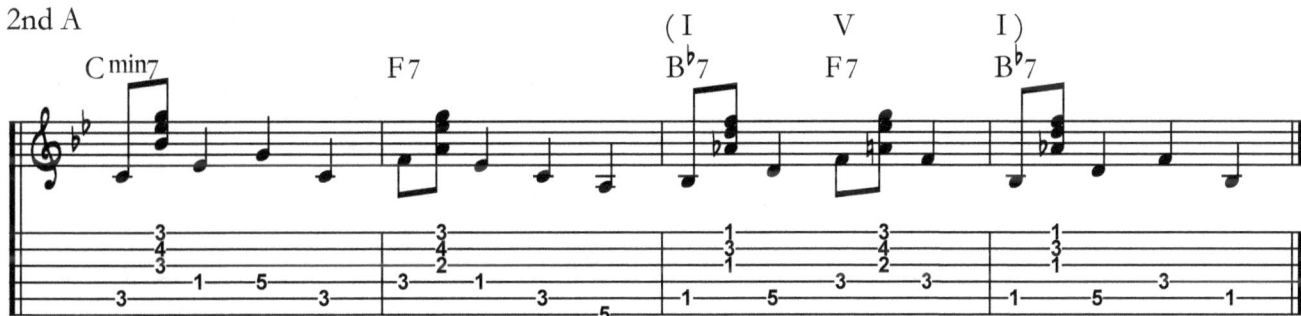

©Waterfall Publishing House 2019

Bb Blues with a Bridge

B Blues with a Bridge

C Blues with a Bridge

D Blues with a Bridge

Eb Blues with a Bridge

E Blues with a Bridge

F Blues with a Bridge

Gb Blues with a Bridge

G Blues with a Bridge

Ab Blues with a Bridge

A Blues with a Bridge

©Waterfall Publishing House 2019

Part 4   THE MINOR BLUES

The Minor Blues is another of the popular jazz standard chord progression. The Minor Blues has an overall "darker" sound than the Major Blues due to the use of the Minor scale tonality.
Often the tonic or I chord will be the Min 6 chord, although there are alternatives which would ultimately be derived from the melody notes. Other options may include the Minor 7 chord or the Minor maj7 chord.
Note that the Minor 6 chord and the Min maj 7 chord are both derived from the Melodic Minor scale, whereas the Minor 7 chord could be Dorian Minor and derived from the Major Scale.

The following chart outlines the Minor Blues progression in D minor.

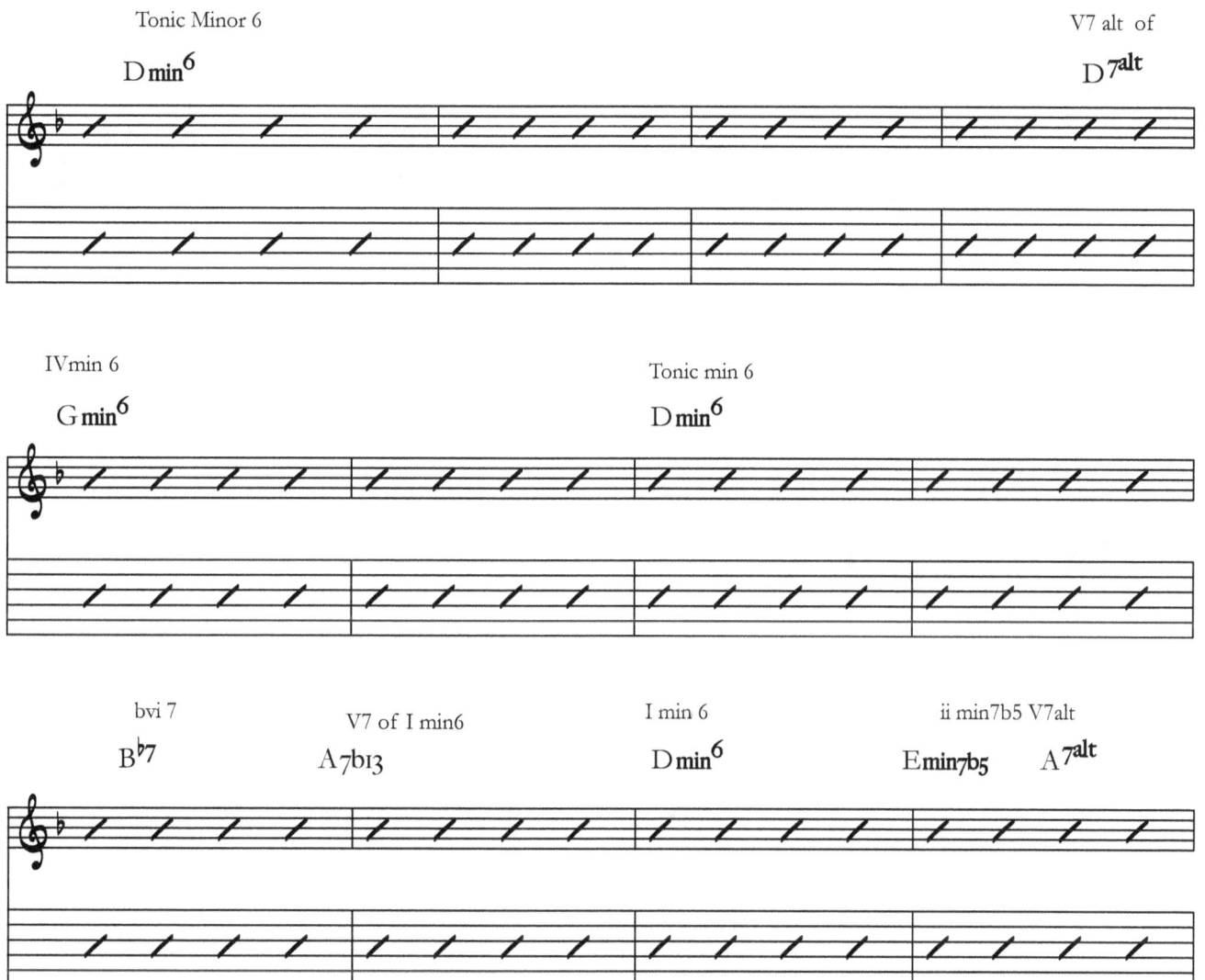

For a more in depth look at chord scale relationships refer to book III in this series Jazz Guitar Workshop - Walking Bass Lines for Guitar - Standard Lines.

D Minor Blues

Eb Minor Blues

E Minor Blues

F# Minor Blues

G Minor Blues

Ab Minor Blues

Bb Minor Blues

B Minor Blues

C Minor Blues

IN CONCLUSION ......

It has been a vast amount of work and dedicated practice that brings the guitarist to the last page of this book, having covered all the examples within.

It has been the aim of the "Jazz Guitar Workshop - Walking Bass Lines" book series to give the aspiring guitarist a solid grounding in how to practice and develop a walking bass accompaniment style in all 12 keys

Having covered the material in this book you are now well on your way to finding your own voice as a musician.

For those of you reading the book that are not familiar with reading treble clef, all examples inside the book have been supplied with tab. Use this as a tool to learn to read the treble clef.

There are many opportunities for the reading musician.

Practice the exercises until they become familiar, striving for good tone, time, and intonation, but most importantly - Listen to as much music as you can, Listen to the masters.

The objective has been to make the material for the student as easy to absorb as possible, as a confidance building mechanism.

Your thoughts and comments are important to us and assist us in providing future generations of musicians with quality educational material.

Thank you
Steven Mooney

Contact us at constructwalkingjazzbasslines@gmail.com

Other books in the series

Constructing Walking Jazz Bass Lines
Jazz Guitar Workshop

Daily Warm Up Exercises for Guitar
by Robert Green
Jazz Guitar Workshop - 12 key Jazz Guitar Workout.
by Robert Green

Walking Bass Lines for Guitar - The Blues in 12 keys
by Steven Mooney
Walking Bass Lines for Guitar - Rhythm Changes in 12 keys
by Steven Mooney
Walking Bass Lines for Guitar - Standard Lines
by Steven Mooney

Constructing Walking Jazz Bass Lines

" Constructing Walking Jazz Bass Lines " Book I
Walking Bass Lines : The Blues in 12 Keys

" Constructing Walking Jazz Bass Lines " Book II
Walking Bass Lines : Rhythm Changes in 12 keys

" Constructing Walking Jazz Bass Lines " Book III
Walking Bass Lines : Standard Lines

" Constructing Walking Jazz Bass Lines " Book IV
Building a 12 Key Facility for the Jazz Bassist Book I

" Constructing Walking Jazz Bass Lines " Book V
Building a 12 Key Facility for the Jazz Bassist Book II

Bass Tablature Series

" Constructing Walking Jazz Bass Lines " Book I
Walking Bass Lines : The Blues in 12 Keys -Bass TAB Edition

" Constructing Walking Jazz Bass Lines " Book II
Walking Bass Lines : Rhythm Changes in 12 Keys - Bass TAB Edition

" Constructing Walking Jazz Bass Lines " Book III
Walking Bass Lines : Standard Lines - Bass TAB Edition

" Constructing Walking Jazz Bass Lines " Book IV
Building a 12 Key Facility for the Jazz Bassist Book I - Bass Tab Edition

Daily Warm Up Exercises for Bass Guitar - Bass Tab Edition

Follow our progress at

Constructingwalkingjazzbaslines.com

Waterfallpublishinghouse.com

©Waterfall Publishing House 2019

www.ingramcontent.com/pod-product-compliance
Lightning Source LLC
Chambersburg PA
CBHW081841170426

43199CB00017B/2805